Animal  Lives

ALLIGATORS AND CROCODILES

Sally Morgan

QEB Publishing, Inc.

First published in the United States by
QEB Publishing, Inc.
23062 La Cadena Drive
Laguna Hills, CA 92653

www.qeb-publishing.com
Reprinted in 2007

Library of Congress Control Number:
2005911036

ISBN 978 1 59566 495 2

Written by Sally Morgan
Designed by Jonathan Vipond
Editor Hannah Ray
Picture Researcher Joanne Forrest Smith

Publisher Steve Evans
Art Director Zeta Davies
Editorial Director Jean Coppendale

Printed and bound in China

Words in **bold** are
explained in the
Glossary on page 31.

Contents

Alligators and crocodiles

This Australian freshwater crocodile has extra-large scales along its back.

Alligators and crocodiles are fierce **predators** that live near water and are the largest of the world's **reptiles**. Reptiles are animals that have skin that is covered with dry **scales**. Most reptiles, including alligators and crocodiles, lay eggs that have leathery shells. Other reptiles include snakes, turtles, and lizards.

Appearance

Alligators and crocodiles look very similar. They both have long bodies and tails, which are covered in thick scales, and legs that stick out to the sides. Most alligators and crocodiles are between 6 and 10 ft. (1.8 and 3 m) in length, with the males being much larger than the females.

Alligator and

The **extinct** crocodile, *Sarcosuchus imperator*, which lived during the time of the dinosaurs, may have reached up to 40 ft. (12 m) in length.

crocodile fact

Both crocodiles and alligators, such as this American alligator, have a long snout with powerful jaws.

Types of alligator and crocodile

Gharials use their long thin snouts to catch fish.

There are 23 different **species**, or types, of alligator and crocodile. They are divided into three families: alligators, crocodiles, and gharials.

The alligator family includes caimans and alligators, which range in size from 3 to 13 ft. (1 to 4 m). The crocodile family includes the saltwater, Nile, New Guinea, and American crocodiles. The gharial family includes just the gharial, which has a very long snout with a pot-like tip.

Telling the difference

The large fourth tooth in the lower jaw of an alligator fits into a socket in the upper jaw and is not visible when the alligator's mouth is closed. In crocodiles, this tooth is visible even when the crocodile's mouth is shut (see right).

Caimans are small and squat, with extremely toothy grins.

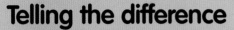

Alligator and crocodile fact

Alligators have between 74 and 80 teeth. As the teeth wear down, they are replaced. An alligator can go through 2000 to 3000 teeth in a lifetime.

Where can you find alligators and crocodiles?

Alligators and crocodiles are found mostly in the **tropical** and subtropical parts of the world.

Alligators are found only in the southeastern United States and in China, while caimans are found mostly in Central and South America. Crocodiles are found in many more places, including Florida, Central and South America, Africa, Pakistan, India, Southeast Asia, and northern Australia. The gharial is found in India, Nepal, Burma, and Pakistan.

8

Alligators and crocodiles often spend the day lying in water to keep cool.

NORTH
AMERICA

ATLANTIC
OCEAN

EUROPE

ASIA

AFRICA

PACIFIC
OCEAN

PACIFIC
OCEAN

SOUTH
AMERICA

INDIAN
OCEAN

AUSTRALIA

Areas where alligators
and crocodiles can be found

ANTARCTIC OCEAN

ANTARCTICA

Wetland habitats

Alligators and crocodiles live in wetland **habitats** such as tropical rainforests, swamps, along rivers, in coastal **mangroves**, and around ocean islands.

Alligator and crocodile fact

Saltwater crocodiles can swim long distances. Some have been found on remote islands in the Pacific, over 800 mi. (1300 km) from other crocodiles.

Although alligators and crocodiles can be found in the same areas, they do not live closely together. For example, in the Florida Everglades, the American crocodile is found near the ocean, where the water is partly salty, while alligators are found farther inland, where the water is fresh.

9

Beginning life

Female alligators or crocodiles lay between 10 and 50 leathery eggs in a nest. Some species dig out a nest in the ground, but others make a mound by using their feet to gather up dirt. Then they lay their eggs inside the mound. By laying her eggs either in the ground or in a mound of dirt, the female makes sure the eggs stay warm.

Alligator and crocodile fact

If the temperature in the nest stays between 89° and 91° F (32° and 33° C), most of the hatchlings will be male. If it is below 88° F (31° C) or above 95° F (35° C), most are female.

This Nile crocodile is laying her eggs in a hole in the ground.

Guarding the nest

Most reptiles abandon their eggs once they have laid them, but female alligators and crocodiles guard their nests and attack any animal that comes too close. They only leave their nests to cool off in the shade or to go for a quick dip in the water. In some species, the males stay close by, too.

Despite the protection, not all the eggs hatch. Predators, such as monitor lizards and bears, raid the nests. Some nests are lost due to flooding, while others get too hot. Disease also kills some baby alligators or crocodiles while they are still in the egg.

These Nile crocodiles
are guarding their eggs.

Hatching

The eggs remain in the nest for between two and three months, depending on the species of alligator or crocodile. Just before hatching, the young alligators or crocodiles inside the eggs make lots of high-pitched sounds. These sounds tell the mother that they are about to hatch. She uses her legs to dig up the nest and help her hatchlings get to the surface. Often, she pushes her snout into the nest to find the eggs.

Hatchlings break out of their eggs by using a special egg tooth at the end of their jaw.

If baby crocodiles are in danger, the mother flips them into her mouth for protection.

Sometimes a hatchling can't break out of its egg. The mother takes the egg gently in her mouth and rolls it backward and forward on her tongue. This opens the shell and allows the hatchling to break free.

Once they have hatched, the mother picks up the hatchlings and carries them to water.

Growing up

The hatchlings stay together after they have hatched. During the day, they spread out to look for food, such as insects and small fish. Their mother is always nearby and she listens for their sounds.

The hatchlings stay with their mother for several months. Young American alligators stay close to their mother for up to two years. When they leave their mother, the young adults move out into the surrounding area.

Alligator and crocodile fact

Only around one percent of young Australian saltwater crocodiles survive to reach adulthood.

Out of every 35 American alligator hatchlings, only six will survive the first year.

Adult crocodiles do not have many enemies but some of the larger species of snake may attack an alligator or a caiman.

Larger is safer

Although young alligators and crocodiles are protected by their mothers, many are killed by predators such as snakes, lizards, birds of prey, hyenas, and tigers. However, the number of alligators and crocodiles killed falls as they get larger. Once they reach a length of three feet (1 m), they are reasonably safe from predators.

Getting around

Alligators and crocodiles can move on land and in water. On land, they either walk slowly, dragging their tails along the ground, or they raise their bodies and tails up off the ground and walk on their toes. Using this "high walk," they can also gallop surprisingly quickly, but only in a straight line and over a short distance because they soon get tired.

Galloping crocodiles can reach speeds of up to 10 mph (17 km/h).

Swimming

Alligators and crocodiles use their long
muscular tails to propel their bodies
through the water. When they swim,
they hold their legs close to the sides
of their body to create a streamlined
shape that glides through the water.

Crocodiles steer
and brake by
sticking out
their legs.

Underwater

Both alligators and crocodiles can float in the water
with just their eyes and nostrils above the water. They
have a flap that closes off their mouths so they can
breathe through their noses. They can dive and stay
underwater for several minutes. Some have been
known to stay underwater for as long as five hours.

17

Senses

Alligators and crocodiles have excellent senses which they use to find their **prey**. They have a special sense that enables them to detect movement in the water. Tiny **sensors** scattered over their face, especially around their mouth, can detect the tiniest **vibrations** caused by animals moving in and around the water.

Alligator and Crocodiles have an extra reflective layer at the back of their eye so they can see more at night. **crocodile fact**

These strange glowing lights on the surface of the water are reflections from the eyes of alligators.

Crocodile eyes

The eyes of these animals are covered by three eyelids. The third eyelid is **transparent** and covers the eye to protect it in the water. Alligators and crocodiles have vertical, cat-like **pupils** that get larger so they can see more in the dark. However, they cannot see much underwater.

Light passes through the black pupil into the eye of the crocodile.

Hunting

Alligators and crocodiles feed on a wide range of animals. Most lie in wait for their prey to pass close by. Some alligators and crocodiles float in the water, while others hide in the vegetation that lies at the water's edge.

This Nile crocodile has caught a gazelle.

Powerful jaws

Alligators and crocodiles grab their prey in their jaws and use their jaws to crush the body of the animal that they have caught. Usually the prey is drowned because the alligator or crocodile dives underwater with its catch.

Alligator and crocodile fact

Each year, crocodiles gather in the Mara River, in Africa, waiting to catch the gnus that cross it on their journey to find fresh grass.

Digestion

Alligators and crocodiles swallow their prey whole or break it up into large pieces. They do not have to eat every day because their bodies use up energy slowly. This means they can survive for several months without food, especially in cooler weather, when they are not so active.

Keeping cool

Reptiles are **ectothermic** animals, which means that their body temperature is similar to that of their surroundings. Crocodiles and alligators are only active when their bodies are warm, so in the morning they lie out in the sun to warm up. During the hottest hours of the day, they either move into the shade or slip into the water to cool down.

Alligators and crocodiles open their mouths to help cool themselves down. This is called gaping.

Crocodiles and alligators lie in the shade during the hottest parts of the day.

Alligator and

When Nile crocodiles bask with their mouths open, birds called Egyptian plovers hop into their mouths and clean the crocodiles' teeth!

crocodile fact

Overheating

After a period of activity, such as running after prey, the alligator or crocodile's body temperature rises and it often overheats. When this happens, it has to cool down by resting in the shade or lying in the water.

23

Living together

Crocodiles and alligators often meet up with other individuals of the same species to form groups. They **bask** in the sun together each day or gather at certain water holes. These groups are mostly females with one or two males. The individuals in these groups can recognize each other by the sounds they make.

Aggressive males

Male crocodiles and alligators don't like many other males around, so larger and older males tend to chase away the smaller males. As a result, younger males usually hang around the outside of a group. During the breeding season, the large males guard their territories and they do not let any other males approach the females in their territory.

Scientists
can tell the age
of a crocodile by looking
at growth rings on
its scales.

This group of female alligators is basking in the sun. When they get too hot, they slip into the water.

Communication

Alligators and crocodiles make a wide range of sounds, including grunts, coughs, growls, and **bellows**. They make a long, loud hiss as a warning before they are going to attack.

Some alligators and crocodiles slap their heads against the water to make a sound that travels a long way, while the gharial makes a popping sound. Many species produce bubbles when they are underwater, and this creates sounds that others can hear.

This Nile crocodile inflates the pouch under its throat to make sounds.

Bellowing alligators

Male alligators bellow to attract a female and to warn off other males. When a male wants to bellow, he raises his head and tail out of the water, waves his tail back and forth, puffs out his throat, and shuts his mouth. Then he vibrates the air in his throat. This creates a vibration in the surrounding water that causes the ground and any other objects in or near the water to vibrate also.

The vibrations are so strong, they make the water "dance" up and down.

Alligator and crocodile fact

Glands under the chin of an alligator or crocodile release a special scent that they use to recognize each other.

Under threat

Alligators and crocodiles are hunted for their skin, which is used to make expensive shoes and handbags. In some places, so many alligators and crocodiles have been hunted that their numbers have fallen to very low levels.

Conservation successes

In 1971, the Australian saltwater crocodile had been hunted almost to extinction. Laws were passed to protect the crocodile, and now its numbers have returned to the levels that existed before hunting started. The numbers of crocodiles in Africa, South America, and North America are increasing, too, due to greater control of hunting.

Farming

Alligator and crocodile farms help to protect alligators and crocodiles living in the wild. This is because the farmed animals provide skins and meat, leaving no reason to hunt wild animals.

In some places crocodiles and alligators are killed for their meat.

Alligator and

Before hunting was controlled in 1970, an estimated 10 million American alligators were killed for their skins.

crocodile fact

29

Life cycle of a Nile crocodile

The female Nile crocodile is ready to breed when she is about 10 years old. She lays between 30 and 80 eggs in a nest, and they hatch two to three months later. She cares for her young for up to two years.

The Nile crocodile lives to be about 40 to 45 years old in the wild, but up to 80 years in captivity.

Hatchling

Juvenile

Full-grown crocodile

Glossary

bask to lie out in the sun

bellow make a roaring sound

ectothermic having a body temperature that is similar to that of the surrounding environment

extinct no longer in existence; disappeared completely

habitat the place in which an animal or plant lives

mangrove a group of tropical evergreen trees that grow closely together in the salty water along a coastline

predator an animal that hunts other animals

prey an animal that is hunted by a predator

pupil the dark spot in the middle of the eye

reptile an animal with dry skin covered in scales. Most reptiles, including alligators and crocodiles, lay eggs

scale a hard flake attached to the skin of an alligator or crocodile

sensor something that detects a stimulus such as a touch, a vibration, or a smell

species a group of animals that look alike and can breed together to produce young

transparent clear; see-through

tropical the parts of the world near the Equator that are hot all year round

vibration a small back-and-forth movement

Index